Erick T. Edwards

# Knockout
## Customer Service

**The Entrepreneur's Guide to
Exceptional Customer Service**

**AYA PUBLISHING**
E-Books

# INTRODUCTION

## Pre-Fight

TRAINING
KNOW YOUR OPPONENT
KNOW THE COMPETITION
THREE MINUTES
ENDURANCE TRAINING
EXPECTATIONS

## Fight Night

Round 1 - THE FIGHT
Round 2 - Exceeding Expectations
Round 3 - Knock out the competition by providing superior CS
Round 4 - THE CORNER
Round 5 - Effective Communication
Round 6 - Direction
Round 7 - Feedback
Round 8 - Active Listening
Round 9 - Concentration
Round 10 - BECOMING A CHAMP
Round 11 - One fight at a time
Round 12 - Continuous Improvement

## Post-Fight

Customers expect more
Competition fights harder
The Rankings
STAYING ON TOP
Don't become Arrogant or Stagnant
Good PR, never forget the fans

# INTRODUCTION

*"Let's get ready to rumble!"*
Michael Buffer

The reality of globalization has taken business strategy and competition to another level; competing for customers takes a tremendous amount of time, effort and resources. However, many companies lose focus and don't take the proper steps at obtaining customers' loyalty. Research shows that 75% of customers actually leave a supplier because of a reason other than dissatisfaction. Creative marketing, efficient processes and streamlining cost are not the only elements of a successful business formula. The buying process is human, human interaction, whether personal or technical, is gauged, graded and scrutinized from every angle at every stage of the process. It's that interaction, we identify as customer service.

For the purpose of this book, I've tried to relate customer service to boxing; a sport where two participants fight each other with their fist, usually gloved. There are three ways to win. Victory is obtained when the opponent is knocked out and unable to get up before the referee counts to ten (a Knockout, or KO) or if the opponent is deemed too injured to continue (a Technical Knockout, or TKO). If there is no stoppage of the fight before an agreed number of rounds, a winner is determined either by the referee's decision or by judges' scorecards.

The term Knockout for the sake of this book does not imply violence against customers. Merriam-Webster's Online Dictionary defines Knockout, the adjective as: *something sensationally striking, appealing, or attractive.* The intention of this book is to share with you the authors' outlook and strategy towards providing sensationally striking, appealing customer service. Boxing has been coined the "Sweet Science" and it's the terminology of that science we're going to incorporate to sweeten up your customer service.

So, now let's address the term "customer service". The term "customer service" in itself is ubiquitous in the area of business. The essence of business is to provide customers with a purchase alternative that leaves the customer satisfied with his/her decision. That satisfaction can be measured or gauged throughout the entire purchasing process and for an extended period after the purchase, in some cases for the life-time of the product or service. Every time a representative of a company has touch time with a customer, customer service is involved.

How does a company classify its service and how do the customers classify the service? Is an agreement between the company and the customer required to validate the classification of service? I'm a fond believer in hard data to corroborate perception. You can claim to be "the greatest" and if your customers think otherwise, who's fooling who? We have to find a way to compare what we think is happening to what is actually happening.

Some companies might use the sophisticated Kano Analysis, which classifies customer preferences into five categories, around 3 attributes. While others develop policies and strategies that foster what the company considers to be a high level of service and accept the fact the results would reflect a bell curve.

Service Curve

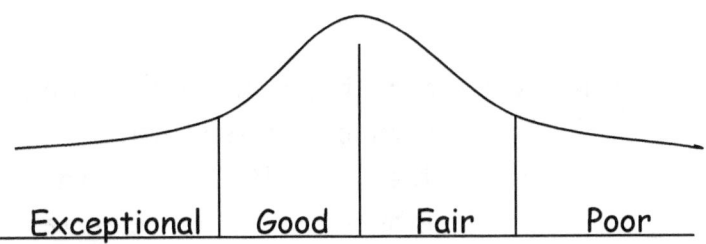

| Exceptional | Good | Fair | Poor |

However, I don't consider this an option. My purpose is to propose an alternative that will position your organization and representatives to confront every customer as an individual and set out to exceed their expectations on every encounter.

Now let's get into the semantics of providing "good customer service"; this implies that there are levels of service provided to customers:

Poor – when a customer has interaction with a representative and the quality of that interaction is deemed *less than* <u>what the customer would have expected from any of your competitors</u>.

Fair – when a customer has interaction with a representative and the quality of that interaction is deemed *nothing but ordinary* <u>having no effect on business transaction.</u>

Good - when a customer has interaction with a representative and the quality of that interaction is *exactly* <u>what the customer expected</u>

Excellent - when a customer has interaction with a representative and the quality of that interaction is *better than* <u>what the customer expected</u>

The million dollar question is; what does the customer expect? Everyone is different and everyone has their unique perspective of what's exceptional, acceptable and what's not. As competition increases the campaign for your customers' business and loyalty becomes more complex. Competitors are offering more and customers are expecting more. The ability to produce or provide a quality product or service is no longer enough to keep a company successful. What we've known as good customer service is steadily becoming; the norm, average, just your regular ole business encounter. More and more companies are willing to go the extra step to obtain and maintain customers. The extra step is also getting further and further away. As expectations become more demanding, the ability to provide excellent service has to be agile.

# TRAINING

*"The fight is won or lost far away from witnesses —
behind the lines, in the gym and out there on the
road, long before I dance under those lights."*
Muhammad Ali

Professional fighters spend most of their
careers training, more so than fighting. They
fight based on unconscious awareness,
awareness learned from training day in and
day out. When techniques become second
nature, the fighter is ready.  The techniques
go from the front of the brain to the back.
She listens to her corner for motivation and
guidance, the more seasoned the fighter
becomes, the less the corner is needed for
guidance.

Training can be split into two areas;
Techniques and Endurance. A boxer has to
train endurance for stamina and strength, to
be prepared to fight 12 rounds. Techniques
are the skills for offense and defense; the
skills need to get the punch in and avoid being
hit.

It's the same in business; endurance training is similar to the training you'd provide an employee for learning products, policies and procedures. Like endurance training

Technique training is the soft skills training. Learning what to say, how to say it and when to say it. The skills of body language, tone of voice, and effective communication are some of the skills addressed in this training.

Very seldom does a seasoned CSR(customer service rep) need to call on her supervisor to solve a complaint. A seasoned CSR knows her tools and has lived the case studies and has learned from experience. How many customers can you afford to lose waiting for all of your CSRs to become seasoned? The shortcut to this involves providing your people with the proper training through real world scenarios and case studies and continuous effective coaching.

As the commitment to training increases and the quality of coaching increases, you can trust the decisions of the CRS to be of quality customer service orientation. One (coaching or training) without the other won't produce the same results. If you invest in training but lack the follow-up, there's a good chance the training won't be put into practice. If you provide tons of coaching and no training the manager and the employee are both going to become frustrated, because the employee will lack understanding of tools and techniques. Imagine teaching a person to drive, giving them a car and telling them to go somewhere they've never been and without a map. On the other hand, giving someone a car, clear directions and a map but they don't know how to drive. These examples are a bit extreme but the point is made. Supervision and coaching provides direction; training facilitates the tools.

## KNOW YOUR OPPONENT (customers' expectations)

Boxer's start their fight preparation according to the intel of their opponent. They learn the style of the opponent, so they can train to counter it.

We can say the same applies to knowing your customer and competition. You may know your customers' names and perhaps where they live. You might even know their buying preferences, but do you know what they think of your product or service; what they think of you or your personnel and most important for the sake of this book, what do they think of their entire interaction with your company, the customer service experience? Many times we fail to ask, we're afraid to ask or don't know how to ask.

Marketing specialist like to throw out words like perception, personalization and appropriateness. What does it mean? Every customer has a mind of his/her own and in that mind there's a world that is unique, there are no two alike. Is it possible to actually satisfy each and every customer? I think yes, I think there's a universal element when it comes to buying something, I like to call it "Buying Truths". These truths start from the very first instance a customer becomes aware of your product or service to the final usage/ the end result of the product or service. These truths include but are not limited to:

- Receiving what you pay for – the product/service presented to you at the time of the sale.
- Paying the price it was offered to you at – no one likes hidden cost.
- The product/service does was it was sold to do.
- The company backs the product/service for the agreed upon time.
- To be treated with respect – respect of your person, time and money.

## KNOW THE COMPETITION

Today's consumer is influenced by their environment more than ever, with information abundance concerning just about everything. They can research store/office hours, guarantees, pricing, product manuals and even comments of others' opinions concerning products and services. You have to put yourself in their shoes and find out what's going on in your area. What are people saying about you, what are they saying about your competition? You need to know. And please don't fall into the "well, the competition is worse" philosophy. The ideal is to "knock your customers out" with excellent service, not just a little better than your competitions' customer service.

It's common to see stores advertising they'll beat or match any other stores price. If they did their research, they wouldn't have to advertise it, everyone would know it.

## THREE MINUTES

Three minutes is the duration of one round of boxing. A boxer trains knowing that each round of the upcoming fight will last 3 minutes and fights are often won and lost in the first 3 minutes. Boxers train to manage themselves within those 3 minutes. We must train to manage ourselves according to time. We can not manage time; it is always the same, 24 hours in a day. However, you can manage yourself within a given frame of time.

A good boxer understands the importance of pacing oneself and utilizing the time given time to implement the fighting strategy. One round is only 3 minutes, but tie 12 rounds of constant fighting and it wears on you. Client after client, issue after issue, and this constant mental battle can take its toll. If you're not prepared, if you take things personally and get frustrated because you do not have the necessary tools, techniques and/or authority, you can wear yourself down mentally and physically.

Like a boxer, we have to focus on and confront task(s) effectively and efficiently. A boxer confronts an opponent; we confront the issues of our clients. It is easy to put an unpleasant situation off for another time. However, when we fail to address these issues right away, we lose an opportunity to show we care and we are concerned. We also risk the possibility of the issue becoming worse.

Train to be prepared and consistent. Major tasks require you to square up and confront them as soon as they come your way, don't put them off. Take the knock out when it's presented; there may not be another opportunity.

# ENDURANCE TRAINING

"It is not enough to do your best; you must know what to do, and then do your best."
W. Edwards Deming

Providing a quality service and / or product is the first step. Knowing your customers and competition is an important second. Now you have the foundation for which you will create your training program.  The program you design for your company will be specific to your findings. However, there is one point that's universal; your program will have to be continuous. Just like road work is an essential part of every boxers training regiment, it establishes endurance. Endurance is important for the long haul.

In business, Continuous Improvement Training Programs (CITPs) are essential for the long haul. It requires constant monitoring of your teams efforts and results; which in turn requires constant modifications of your program and standards. I use the word standard with hesitation because for me the word standard implies conformity and it's conformity that we don't want. Perhaps the term "standard minimal", meaning the least acceptable outcome would be more appropriate. The customer left satisfied but we failed to "knock'em out".

A boxer is happy to win a fight, whether by decision or knockout. In the world of business, we need the knockout. It's the knock out that's going to take the company to the next level.

Your CITPs will start with a mission statement. Your mission statement should be written by your team with your guidance. This is the philosophical statement that will drive your team and when they've helped to create it, they have a vested interest in seeing that it succeeds.

Darden Restaurants, the world's largest company-owned and operated full service restaurant company, mission statement is "We take pride in providing a terrific dining experience to every guest, every time, in every one of our restaurants. That is how we will be the best company in casual dining, now and for generations." One of the company's core values is "Being "of service" which states "Being of service is our pleasure. We treat people as special and appreciated by giving of ourselves, doing more than expected, anticipating needs, and making a difference." That might help explain why company served over 404 million meals in fiscal 2009. You can believe a lot of those were return customers.

Boxers have consistent careers when they have good corners. Corners are the management teams that make sure the boxer stays with the strategy and also have the insight to communicate change when necessary. When the corner observes that the opponent has changed styles, it has to communicate a new strategy to the boxer. When you see that something in the environment has changed the elements for which your team has trained, you have to be able to communicate a new strategy to your team. The team needs to understand the importance of being flexible when change is necessary. In additional to being continuous, training has to emphasize change and communication. The CITPs have to be agile and aligned to the business strategy.

# THE FIGHT

"I'm scared every time I go into the ring, but it's how you handle it. What you have to do is plant your feet, bite down on your mouthpiece and say, 'let's go.'"
Mike Tyson

Boxing is often called the "Sweet Science" but if you're on the wrong end of the glove it's more like "Bitter Logic". When confronted with a fight; winning is the desired outcome, knocking the opponent out is the icing on the cake and the sooner the better. A boxer, who knocks her opponent out in the early rounds, not only goes home early but has put less wear and tear on her body. She also builds a reputation as being a knock out artist, a powerful foe and someone to be respected in the ring.

In business, the first objective is to fulfill a need, usually by providing a product or service. The strategy for providing this product or service takes into account customers' expectations, customers' alternatives and how to make the offering known. Once the business has fulfilled the customers' needs in a way that keeps them coming back, the fight is won; impressing your customers enough to become advocates of your business, referring friends and family; that's the knock out, the icing on the cake. In order to accomplish that, customers' issues should be dealt with quickly, go for the knock out right away when possible. By providing solutions, efficiently and effectively the company builds a reputation; a reputation that fosters repeat customers and referrals.

## Go for the KO

Don't be afraid of going for the quick knock out. Numerous primetime, big money fights have been won and lost in the first 3 minutes.

This is best for experienced people, who know their business inside out. It's like the FAQ section of a website. After you've been in the business for a while, certain complaints, problems or issues will tend to be more frequent and the solutions for those issues are generally the same. Your experience, knowledge and training will allow you to solve these situations with sharp and precise decision making, a KNOCK OUT! Allowing the client to go on with their lives, feeling pleased with you, the experience and most important your company/organization.

Maya Angelou once said: "I've learned that people will forget what you said, people will forget what you did, but people will never forget how you made them feel."

When you've determined that a quick KO isn't possible, you have to change the strategy and fast.

## Cut-Off the Ring

Keeping control of your environment is important and to some extent key in fostering a customer satisfying experience. Fighters are taught techniques to stop their opponents from running or dancing around the ring. Commonly fighters try to avoid punches or avoid direct confrontation with a physically stronger fighter by dancing, also known as using the ring.

Cutting off the ring will allow you to keep your customer focused on specific issues and solutions. It's not unheard of for customers to be side-tracked by previous past experiences and/or anticipated objections to their desired outcome.

Maintain engagement, keep eye contact, paraphrase or summarize. Use effective communication skills, such as, respectively interrupting a customer who is venting and has gotten off track and is not allowing you to get a word in. The person has to take a breath; listen carefully, jump in, excuse the interruption, and summarize what the issue is or paraphrase the relevant information you've been given. Ask the customer, "Did I understand correctly?"

## The Ole One Two

You've most likely heard the term, "Hit'em with the ole One-Two". In boxing it refers to a left jab followed by a right, at least for right handed fighters. In the customer service ring, I'm going to refer to it as a smile followed by a solution.

A smile is important, there's nothing worse than having to go back to a service or product provider because of a defect, malfunction, mistake or misunderstanding and being confronted by someone with an attitude, regardless if you're right or wrong. Your purchase was made in good faith; your money was accepted in good faith, so it's natural that you expect to be attended in good faith, concerning after purchase issues.

Let's keep in mind that a solution doesn't necessarily mean the preferred outcome of the customer. A win-win situation is always ideal, however not always possible. A solution is an outcome that is set out to be satisfactory for all parties involved and if that's not the case, it should be first and foremost, a logically outcome. Many companies have a no questions asked refund policy, but does that always solve the issue? If the person needs a product or service and perhaps the one you initially sold them isn't the solution and you refund their money, their initial need remains. A refund policy is always good; however employees should always attempt to provide a solution for initial need first, once it's determined that the company can not fulfill the clients need, then a refund should be offered, when applicable.

Confront Your Opponent (Customer), not in a confrontational manner but in a receiving manner.   A manner that says, I'm here to assist you. Notice I wrote assist, not help. You offered a product / service, the client trusted you and purchased, but something didn't happen as the client expected and now the ball is back in your court or should I say the fight has began.

Be there 100%, listen without any predetermined opinion. Be careful not to jump the gun with a perceived solution. If you knock the client down and not out, you've lost a valuable opportunity for a knock out and it may just make things worse. So read body language, read between the lines (intonation), listen for pauses and know when to step in and suggest a solution or ask for more information. If you find yourself in a bind and you can't come up with a solution or maybe you don't have authority for the proper corrective measure, then you need to wrap your opponent up. In boxing, often one boxer will grab and hold the other, in a way where the other boxer can no longer through punches. The referee has to step in and separate the two. In business we'll use this method, to stall and take the opportunity to build a relationship with the client. And again, communication is the key.

## Counter Punch

"Getting hit motivates me. It makes me punish the guy more. A fighter takes a punch, hits back with three punches."
Roberto Duran

A counter-attack begins immediately after an opponent throws a punch, exploiting the opening in the opponent's position.

Many believe a good defense is the best offense. The fighter, Floyd Mayweather jr. at the time of this writing is undefeated with a record of 43-0, 26 by knockout. He's not known as a power puncher but he's considered to have one of the best defenses of all time. He uses a defense technique similar to the Philly Shell Defense. The technique requires the defensive fighter to keep a low left hand facing the opponent, inviting a right hand shot, triggering a right hand counter punch.

One form of "Counter Punching" in business is turning a compliant into business.

Salespeople use the technique of up-selling to get a perspective buyer to purchase a better class / grade of product or service, and/or to purchase a complimentary item. Everyone in your company should be a salesperson, everyone who has contact with the client and especially customer service employees. When someone comes in or calls to complain, confront the issue provide a solution and offer a complimentary item / service, counter punch, when appropriate.

A whole strategy became famous based on the concept of counter punching, the "rope-a-dope".

## Rope-A-Dope

On October 30, 1974 the Rumble in the Jungle took place. It was a fight between then heavy weight champion George Foreman and the contender, Muhammad Ali. This fight was an historical event for boxing. George Foreman was the favorite and he clearly out matched Ali in size and power. However, boxing is not just size and power; it's also strategy and technique. At that fight, Ali introduced to the boxing world, the rope-a-dope. The rope-a-dope is a strategy where a boxer assuming a protected stance, lying against the ropes, and allowing his opponent to hit him, in the hope that the opponent will become tired and make mistakes which the boxer can exploit in a counter attack.

Rope-a-dope customer service refers to allowing the customer to complain; let them vent, but listen attentively. By listening attentively you'll accomplish several things; you'll get to the root of the customer's issue, you'll most likely find out what the client's need is, the cause of their dissatisfaction and you'll know what the client expects from you.

Each person lives in a mini world, which revolves around them, within the world we all share. They all have different expectations of your product / service and how you're expected to respond to their complaints, making the KO that much more complicated. How are you supposed to know what's expected of you, you don't read minds. That's where the art of communication comes into play; listening intensively and knowing when to respond, the counter punch.

Knowing when to step in is a crucial factor in obtaining a knock out. The way of knowing when requires concentration. You may have a million things going on in your world, but when you face off with a client you have to concentrate. In many cases you have to let the client vent. The product didn't work, wasn't the correct one, or maybe there was a misunderstanding; regardless the fight has started. So as you listen for the reason why, you have to come up with a solution and keep it to yourself until the client finishes the flurry (rope-a-dope). It's important to not come to any premature conclusions, so you have to continue listening even though you may think you already have the solution. You can add fuel to the fire by stepping in too soon, leaving yourself open to be Knocked out, losing a valuable client.

After the customer has vented and your window of opportunity opens, you have to step in with a concise solution. Your words should have an understanding intonation, but yet with the authority to provide a solution.

# THE CORNER (Coaching)

*"I just put the reflexes in the proper direction."*
Angelo Dundee

Men like Angelo Dundee, Emanuel Stewart and Lou Duva have had great boxing careers, but not as fighters, as trainers. They're known for helping to create some of the greatest boxers in the history of the sport. Often the difference between a good boxer and a champ is the trainer. These are the guys that put the boxers through the training regiments and they teach the techniques necessary for success. There's another important role that trainers play, it's coaching from the corner. They're in the corner analyzing the opponents' every move, looking for an opportunity and then communicating that opportunity to their fighter. Equally as important, they analyze what their fighter is not doing, when she is not following the planned strategy.

Boxers aren't considered to be scholars, no disrespect intended but I think this is common knowledge, and often we feel the same way about other professionals. It takes a good leader to consistently achieve with people in general; it takes an excellent leader to consistently achieve with people who aren't expected to be achievers.

The manager of a business, like a boxing manager has to have a strategy, the analytical skills to make sure the strategy is on track, the communication skills to provide feedback and the leadership skills to set a new course when necessary. The manager coaches from the corner, giving the encouragement, feedback and recognition when necessary. That ability to motivate and touch the right buttons at the right time.

## Communication

In 2009, the then WBC (World Boxing Council) titleholder, super middleweight champion Carl Froch trailed 106-102 on two of the judges' scorecards entering the final round, but he delivered a stunning knockout of Jermain Taylor in the final round with less than a minute remaining make a comeback and win the fight.

Going into the 12th and final round, Froch's trainer, Robert McCracken to his fighter that he was losing the fight and he had to have a really big 12th round. As simple as it may seem, those words put the urgency necessary in Froch to give it all he had. If McCracken had said, "you're doing good out there champ, just keep at him" Froch would have surely lost on decision.

Telling people what they want to hear is not necessarily best for them. A lazy manager/coach can also be guilty of telling people what they want to hear, because they haven't taken the time to analyze the true situation and therefore it's easier just to keep the current path.

There are two adages that come to mind when I think about communication; "communication is a two way street" and "it's not what you say, it's how you say it".

Effective communication is vital for the success of personal interactions and for organizational communication. Client facing employees are not only the face of the organization, they're also the voice.

Therefore, it's important to choose your words carefully and always be clear and precise. When confronted by a client who has an issue, we don't want to add fuel to the fire. Don't assume that others know or understand the obvious. Let's avoid misinterpretation and misunderstandings.

## What Did You Say? – It's Not Just the Words

Studies have shown that very little of what is communicated between people is transmitted through words. I've seen figures around 10%.

However, choice of words is important and often how you phrase a sentence matters. A slight change can change a person's perception of you, from polite and caring to rude and obnoxious.

Which one sounds better?

How can I help you? or How can I be of service to you?

What do you want me to do? or What would you like me to do?

I can't do that! or Unfortunately I don't have the authority to do that.

Do ABC. or Would you mind doing ABC.

That's not the way it's done. or Have you considered doing it this way?

Again, it's not just the words; it's also how you say them. Now, let's couple the words with the tone of voice.

Around 40% of communication comes through the tone of the voice, the tempo, and the volume.

Consider the powerful effect that tone of voice can have on the meaning of a sentence. When said in a strong tone of voice, listeners might interpret approval and enthusiasm. The same words said in a hesitant tone of voice might convey disapproval and a lack of interest.

Inflection is another important characteristic of the voice. The pitch and speed at which you speak has a big influence on how the receiver interprets what you're saying.

## *Feedback*

Great Feint, Great Knockout!

In 1987, the Light Middleweight (weight division from 147 to 154 pounds) match between Donald Curry and Mike McCallum had been anticipated by many boxing aficionados. McCallum was known as a body puncher, and of course he used this to his advantage. Curry on the other hand was a fantastic technical boxer, very nice to watch and one the purists especially enjoyed. The clash of styles was going to be very interesting!

Curry had a bad habit of dropping his hands and leaning back slightly when seeing an uppercut, almost 'relaxing' out of the way. McCallum had noticed this, either during the fight or in his pre-fight preparations, and tried earlier on in the fight to feint an uppercut and land a left hook. Despite the best efforts of McCallum, Curry had boxed brilliantly to hold the lead and was in a very strong position.

In the 5th round however, McCallum feinted a right uppercut to the body and unloaded with a tremendous long range left hook, connecting squarely on the side of Curry's jaw. OK, Donald Curry could be accused of losing concentration at long range, but McCallum's tactical observation was most definitely the primary factor in the knock out.

So what's a feint? Feinting is body movement or an incomplete attack used primarily to create reactions. The idea is to create an opening or to draw the opponent into responding so you may anticipate and counter.

Boxing is as physical as any sport can be and reading body language is a major part of it.

Body language is a major factor in communication. It's believed that over 50% of communication is made by body language, unless you're on the phone of course. Any many people believe that your tone during a telephone conversation can be influenced by your posture, while on the phone.

While the boxer often uses her body to confuse her opponent, the CRS will use her body to communicate openness and read the body language of the listener to interpret attitude or acceptance.

Here are a few things to keep in mind:

1. **Don't cross your arms or legs** – This helps to avoid the appearance of being defensive or guarded.

2. **Make eye contact, but don't stare** - By making eye contact it shows sincerity, however you don't want to stare, it may make the person feel uneasy.

3. **Sit up Straight** - If you're sitting and talking with someone, sit up straight and lean forward. It shows that you're interested in what they have to say.

4. **Relax** – If you look tense, it makes others tense and they may lose confidence in your ability to provide a solution. Don't fidget.

5. **Facial Expressions** – the implications taken from a risen eye brow, one eye squinted, movement of your lips and nostrils can vary from culture to culture. Keeping a sincere smile goes a long way.

**6. Head Movement** – knowing when to nod your head in agreement or disagreement is an important tool in communication.

**7. Hand Movement** – people are often descriptive with their hands. But don't use them to much or it might become distracting.

**8. Mirroring** –To make the connection better you can try a bit of proactive mirroring. If he leans forward, you might lean forward. If she holds her hands on her thighs, you might do the same. But don't react instantly and don't mirror every change in body language. There can be a fine line between mirroring and mocking.

## Active Listening

Depending on the study, it's believed that listeners only take in 25-50% of what they hear.

Opened ended questions are great for getting people to talk and divulge information. However, if you're like most people, you don't get the most of the information because your mind is occupied with thinking about what you're going to say when it's your turn. Put your own ego on hold. Learn to really listen to what people actually are saying.

When you start to really listen, you'll receive tons of information that will allow you to either ask deeper diving questions or you'll get to the root of the concern right away.

Active listening involves reading between the lines, catching implications and innuendos. I remember my teachers in school saying, "please give me your undivided attention", but they never explained what that meant. Many of us thought it meant, not talking to someone else while he/she was talking and not looking out the window. However, while we were looking directly at the teacher, our minds were at recess on the play ground and as we got older, our minds were off on social excursions.

It would have been a good idea to explain to us that by "undivided attention" he/she meant actively listening, and you do that by:

- Concentrating on what is being said, no distractions.

- Like with reading, it's not just the words, understand meaning and context.
- Mentally try paraphrasing what you hear into your own words.
- Provide feedback by nodding in agreement or disagreement when appropriate.
- Don't draw conclusion or start building a rebuttal until the speaker has finished speaking.
- It's important to stay conscious of your active listening strategy.

## Coaching

*"I never teach until I've spoken to the fighter. I have to first determine his emotional state, get his background, to find out what I have to do, how many layers I have to keep peeling off so that I get to the core of the person so that he can recognize, as well as I, what is there."* **Cus D'Amato**

Whether it's sports coaching or professional coaching, the ideal of facilitating /aiding /assisting someone to reach a certain level of performance or goal is the same. There are different forms of coaching styles, frameworks and facilitating methodologies.

The key is to adapt a style that best suits you and your audience.

Understand the barriers to coaching. People learn, think and communicate differently. Adopting a style to meet the different personalities within your organization most likely won't come off-the-shelf and won't be easy. You have to find the right words, terms, and phrases that you feel comfortable with, because if people perceive your conversation as scripted, they won't consider you sincere. If you come across as insincere, then good luck with earning their trust and getting their buy in. There will be trial and error, but when you're conscious of your strategy and receptive to feedback, the errors don't have to be career ending, neither yours nor theirs.

The previous paragraphs in this section have good insight into effective communication. Effective communication is an essential part of Coaching. Knowing when to listen, when to talk, what to say and how to say it, allows a coach to gain trust and show integrity.

Here are some phrases you should try to avoid:

- I told you so.
- Don't do it that way.
- What's wrong with you?
- Are you SOS (stuck on stupid)
- You're not right for that assignment.
- You can't do it.
- Don't be a baby.
- You want this job, don't you?
- It's my way or the highway.
- Why are you always late?

Instead try using:

- Have you considered doing it this way...
- Help me understand ...
- What can I do to help you ...
- Is there anything I can do to assist you with ...
- Let's leverage your strengths to ...
- You're a valued employee and we need you to ...

Old habits are hard to break and new habits form with repetition. Training and practice are keys to building positive habits for both management and client facing employees. Coaching done correctly reinforces targeted behavior. When people are accustomed to doing things the right way and their good habits are second nature. Chances are they'll respond the right way under pressure.

# BECOMING A CHAMP

*"When they commit to doing something, they commit. There's no holding back."*
Don King

We have established the importance of training and coaching. One without the other doesn't result in becoming a champ. A quality combination of the two creates a synergy that allows your CSR to thrive. Boxers persist in the beginning, looking / waiting for their big shot, a title bout. Once they get that shot they have to perform. There's no one "big shot" for organizations, the championship is won over time with every encounter with a customer. Organizations don't have the opportunity for a lucky punch. The competition is heavy, aggressive and numerous; ready to pounce on your lack luster performance, mistakes and conformity. There's no belt (extravagantly designed belt used to signify the champion), just profit, success or failure.

We generally start by looking at the big picture, the fight. Champions are made one round at a time. Successful companies are made one customer at a time.

In the world of boxing, there's a winner and a loser. In the business world, we seek win-win scenarios. If the customer must lose, we must master the art of allowing them to save face.

Examples:

> "Sorry, we can't provide you with a refund for that item, however we can give you credit to be used on any other item in store"
>
> or
>
> "I understand the quality didn't meet your expectations, we'd really appreciate it if you posted a comment on our website, to let others know about your experience. I'd also like to extend a discount for one with perceived better quality."

When the business wins and the customer loses, it's often a short term win, the round is won. If the customer never returns and talks negatively about his/her experience to friends, family, blogs and colleagues. The negative impact will greatly outweigh the short term win. Too many rounds like that and the fight will definitely be lost.

**One fight at a time** (one customer at a time)

By staying consistent with training and coaching you will insure quality and reliability.

What can you expect from your CRSs in the area of autonomy? I've developed the Service Boxing Ring Model to address just that.

## Customer Service
## Boxing Ring Model
(CSR Autonomy)

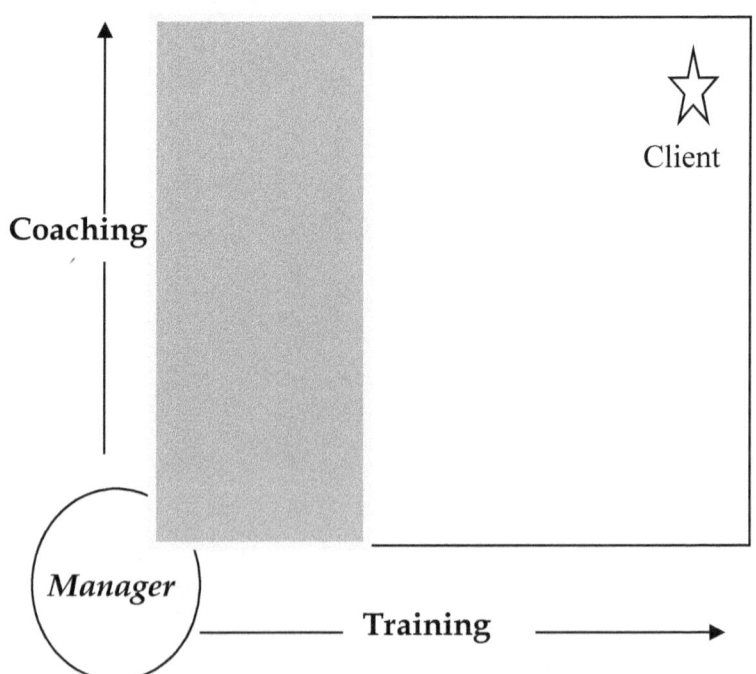

Very seldom are there times when extremes play a role in customer service. For example it's rare that you will find a situation where there's lot's of supervision and no training. In this scenario the leadership is more so to blame than the CSR. I have seen cases of this in small family owned businesses where someone in the family is always around supervising, I use the term lightly; however the staff hasn't been given any training what so ever. The CSR is hired, given a title, maybe a job description and set out to perform the task. The person actually learns the job through 100% trial and error; errors promptly pointed out by the supervisor. The CSR lacks authority and often lacks knowledge of processes and procedure.

So what happens when the supervisor isn't present? The CSR simply replies NO to everything. The customer gets frustrated because logic and sympathy are not taken into consideration.

# Customer Service
# Boxing Ring Model
(CSR Autonomy)

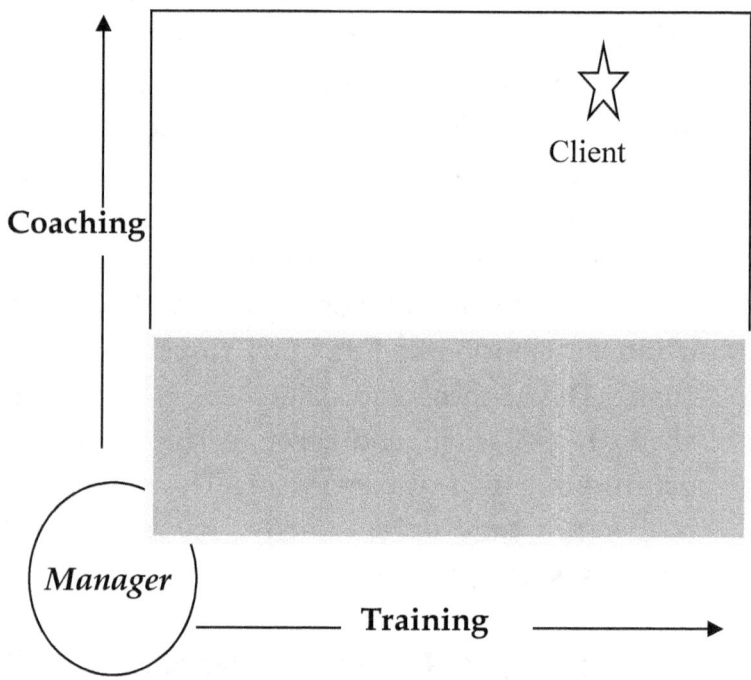

In contrast to the previous example, here's a scenario where the organization has invested lots of time and money in training but pays very little attention or gives little value to coaching.

Training will generally take place in three areas, soft skills, product/service knowledge and processes. This type of organization usually understands the importance of innovation and people development.

The major issue with a concentration of effort on training, without proper coaching, revolves around behavior and peoples' general disposition to resist change. We sometimes need to be reminded of desired behavior. Organizations will also sometimes send the front line CSR to training and leadership is involved in the training. They may be involved with the selection, but they don´t actually participate. Here, we've armed the soldier with a gun and the officer has no battle plan. If the coach doesn't know what was covered in the sessions or lacks the know how to implement the recently gained techniques. The CSR comes back with ideals and enthusiastic to be confronted with supervision that's not on the same page. This model creates frustration and conformity for the CSR.

Believe it or not processes can also be a root of frustration. Processes are established for standardization and consistency; it helps to set clear expectations on both parts. We try to group situations and scenarios, which will allow us to apply a certain process that provides a solution/desired outcome for both parties. However, processes should never become an obstacle to success. What happens when the situation or scenario is slightly different?

# Customer Service
# Boxing Ring Model
## (CSR Autonomy)

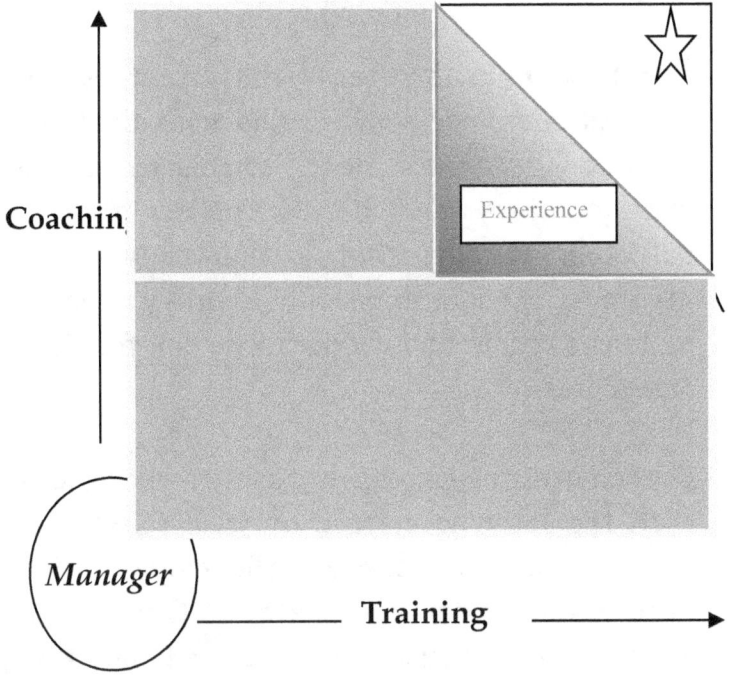

It's easy to say we want a customer oriented culture in our businesses, but to foster that culture, we have to nurture our CRSs with the necessary training and coaching. When we find the right combination, we're on the road to success. This model shows that a CRS who has received an adequate amount of training, paired with consistent quality coaching will have the ability to excel alone. The person will have the capacity to conjure the two, add it to personal/professional experiences and originate solutions deemed win-win.

Start with a strategy that fosters the desired customer service, Knockout Customer Service. Establish clear communication of that strategy and desire. Follow that by selecting training that is aligned with the strategy. Leadership will identify subject matter experts and vendors who can facilitate the topics.

Coordinate training in a fashion that works with the learning culture of your CSRs. That would include style/methodology, time, duration and delivery method. Options can vary from; in-house designed and delivered, having a consulting company identify and work with in-house subject matter experts to develop customized training, to vendors who have off the self trainings and/or seminars. Nowadays, training can even take place virtually or through web based offerings.

Communicate the importance of the training and how it aligns with the success of the organization. Recognize participants for attending. Create the understanding that the new tools they've acquired are supported by management and their implementation is deemed necessary and important.

Leadership has to not only be aware of the trainings, but also has to become an advocate of them. The leaders have to coach the participants to use the newly acquired knowledge/techniques. Evaluation of the effectiveness of training is important to determining the ROI. Not everything can be measured, especially when we're talking about behavior. However, when the strategy aligns with company goals, the bottom line is one way and customer feedback is another.

## Celebrate

Don't forget to celebrate. Boxing champions are known for their lavish celebrations. It's part of the bragging rights of being champion. Reward CSRs for giving KO service. A robust employee appreciation and recognition program is a most. The idea of not rewarding people because they're getting paid to do a job won't foster a culture of Knock Out Customer Service.

The Society of Human Resources Management (SHRM)'s 2012 survey showed that only 29% of employees surveyed were satisfied with the level of recognition they receive for doing a good job at work. I refer to this survey in order to emphasize the importance of people wanting to be recognized for a job well done. Undoubtedly monetary reward is the reward most employees prefer, however the lack of monetary resources shouldn't discourage management from recognizing employees. According to a poll developed by Accountemps in 2012; "Thirty-five percent of workers and 30 percent of chief financial officers (CFOs) polled cited frequent recognition of accomplishments as the most effective nonmonetary reward." A pat on the back can go a long way and who doesn't appreciate recognition in front of one's peers. Management has to feel the pulse of what works for its employees. Generic employee programs may not work and may actually have the opposite effect. Management also benefits by using the opportunity to model and reinforce the desired behavior.  This is the type of behavior we want and we're willing to reward/recognize those who deliver.

# STAYING ON TOP

*"The man who views the world at 50 the same as he did at 20 has wasted 30 years of his life."*
Muhammad Ali

It's not an easy road becoming a champ and staying champ may even be harder. It's a formula that requires the fighter (CSR) and coach (manager) to be on the same page. It also means never becoming complacent. Don't take success for granted and definitely don't take your clients for granted.

On February 11, 1990, Buster Douglas shocked the world by knocking out Mike Tyson. Tyson was a huge betting favorite, but Douglas was at an emotional peak after losing his mother to a stroke 23 days prior to the fight, and fought the fight of his life. Douglas had a 12-inch reach advantage over Tyson and he kept his jab in Tyson's face all night. Tyson being Tyson caught Douglas with an uppercut in the eighth round and sent him to the canvas. However, Douglas made it to his feet and was able to keep fighting. And fight he did; he beat Tyson for the next two rounds. Starting the 10th round, Douglas unleashed a brutal combination of hooks that sent Tyson to the canvas for the first time in his career. The knockout victory by Douglas over Tyson, the previously undefeated and undisputed champion, has been described as one of the most shocking upsets in boxing history.

It's easy to take success for granted and it's just as easy to fall from grace. You can't let your guard down. A well devised strategy to stay focused should be an integral part of your overall strategy for success.

## Continuous Improvement (Innovation)

Discipline to continuously work at pleasing your customers will make your service consistently good. Dedication to being number one will require you to continuously seek better processes and improved communication.

### Competition fights harder

Once you're on top, the competition will start imitating you and in many cases will attempt to do what you do, better. You have to keep moving, keep changing and keep innovating. Setting previous success as a baseline for improvement and constantly raising the bar. Setting realistic goals is part of the process, however knowing when and how to set stretch goals will make the difference.

There's no doubt, the better your service, the more your clients began to expect. They've always received great service from your organization and they've recommended you to all their friends and family. How is it that your competition is doing X and you haven't one-up'ed them, when logically feasible.


## The Rankings

Boxing has different organizations that provide rankings and polls of boxers based on weight class. Each organization has it politics and processes for ranking a fighter, so it's no surprise that the rankings between organizations are often different.

A ranking of employees serves no purpose other than competition, for programs such as employee of the month. What is it we want from our client facing employees and how can we break that down into measurable units?

I have heard managers say, we have good or bad customer service, and I always ask "how do you know?" Often they'll give an example or two, and my reply is "how do you gauge improvement based on that?" You need a concrete baseline, something to measure against in order to measure real improvement.

Not every customer interaction is easy to measure. Call Centers measure practically every aspect of their client facing employees' activities. Measurement is important because it allows us to analyze key/critical performance indicators, which in turn allows us to make decisions concerning who needs what training and prioritize training resources. If you don't have an automated way of measuring your KPIs (Key Performance Indicators) than perhaps you'll have to email surveys, encourage customers to make comments or even call.

Measuring behavior is no easy task; especially areas like intention, knowledge, skills, and self-efficacy.

## Don't become Arrogant / Don't become Stagnant

*"To succeed at the pinnacle of the sport, boxers need to be as good at fighting outside the ring, as they are in it. It's crucial the top boxers 'talk the talk' as well as 'walk the walk', which sits hand in hand with the natural arrogance needed to rise to the top of boxing."*

The list of boxers accused of being arrogant would cover an entire unit in this book. After all, how did Muhammad Ali become known as "The Greatest"?

He walked the talk. Like in boxing, a business has to back up its claims with performance. Unlike boxing, fans/clients don't like arrogant businesses, or dealing with arrogant CSRs. If you have a business that's successful and you treat your customers like you have the last bottle of water and they need you and you're still successful; please let me know where you're located so I can set up across the street.

I've seen situations where certain companies have a significant market advantage, unique product/service, or an illegal (but not public) agreement with its other 2 or 3 competitors and the service is horrendous. The receptionist ignores you, the sales person keeps you waiting and the manager won't give you the time of day. The item is delivered or the service is installed whenever the person handling it just happens to be in your area, despite the date you've been told. And if you don't like it, well do without it.

Fortunately, globalization has created an environment where everyone needs to up their game.

Every business depends on a client, no matter how attractive the item or service; no matter how cheap or small the profit margin. Even nonprofit organizations need donations. Without the clients there are no sales/donations, without sales/donations there is no income.

Managers have to be very careful not to create an environment of arrogance from the top down. You want people to have confidence in you, you're employees and you're organization. It's very important that you're employees have confidence in themselves. However, confidence should never be mistaken for arrogance.

# Good PR, never forget the fans

(Community Involvement)

*"Service to others is the rent we pay for our room here on earth!"*
Muhammad Ali

Community Involvement is not to be confused with Community Service. Mike Tyson had to do 200 hours of community service as part of a punishment for a crime he was found guilty of. Community Involvement is voluntary and genuine. Boxing Champs are often recognized around the world. A lot of it has to do with the promotions around the fights, which are multimillion dollar events. Needless to say, some fighters become global celebrities. Not only do we follow their boxing careers, we also follow their personal lives. So when they use their money or time for the good of the community, it's recognized.

Former Heavy-weight champ Lennox Lewis received a lot of publicity for a public service announcement against domestic violence. It was obvious he wasn't trying to promote his next fight by doing so, and this is the type of genuine involvement that people recognize and admire.

Manny Pacquiao created a foundation which focuses on education for the poor. Pacquiao himself had dropped out of high school because of extreme poverty. He is loved by millions in his home country of the Philippines, not so much because of this greatness in the ring but because he has never forgotten where he came from and gives time, not just money, but time to the community.

Community involvement isn't required of a boxer. These champions often make millions of dollars, and they do so because of the fans. Some of them feel the need to give back. It's true they have the skills that we like to see, just like a company has the product or service that we need or desire. But without the fans paying their hard earned money to see the fight, there wouldn't be the payday. Without the customer patronizing your product or service over your competitors, there would be no profits.

Showing appreciation to the community can take various forms; from donating money to local charities to sponsoring a little league team. Companies will often develop global programs and partner with other global community programs. Some companies encourage and reward employees for volunteer service.

How is this relevant to Knockout Customer Service? The entire business process is holistic, from the beginning bell to the end of the final round, the final bell. From making the client aware of your existence, through the sale to post service, it's all one experience to the client in the end. Your clients' perception of your company is also holistic. I conducted a survey where 85% of the participants believed that any company that does right by the community, will also do right by its clients. Doing right in the community, means giving back and community involvement. It's no longer enough to provide jobs in the community, the business and the community grows together. The well being of the community helps the clients and the business.

Thank you for taking the time to read this book. I hope you enjoyed the boxing analogies. The idea was to put a different twist on something you're most likely already familiar with; a refresher on putting clients first and making sure your team is equipped with the right tools and techniques to keep your customers coming back.